Seed Soil
Feed Soul

Seed Soil Feed Soul

An Introduction to the Benefits of Gardening Naturally

Aiden M Bertolino-Haley

Tampa, Florida

The content associated with this book is the sole work and responsibility of the author. Gatekeeper Press had no involvement in the generation of this content.

Seed Soil: Feed Soul:
An Introduction to the Benefits of Gardening Naturally

Published by Gatekeeper Press
7853 Gunn Hwy., Suite 209
Tampa, FL 33626
www.GatekeeperPress.com

Library of Congress Control Number: 2024951682

ISBN (hardcover): 9781662959844
eISBN: 9781662959851

For my father, Daniel Haley,
the first gardener I ever met and my first teacher. He has
always encouraged me to read and to write in spite of our
mutual dyslexic condition.

Table of Contents

Introduction

The purpose of writing this book is twofold. Firstly, I just needed a way to begin to solidify some ideas I have had brewing inside for quite some time. Secondly—and probably more importantly—I wanted to encourage you, the reader, to consider planting a garden or, if you already have one, simply spend more time out in it. I invite anyone who picks up this book to reconsider their own relationship to nature and to play with preconceived ideas about their ability to serve the natural world.

The structure of the book evolved naturally out of my split interests, so naturally, the bulk of it is split into two parts, each with two chapters and preceded by a brief autobiography to set the scene at the start. The first conceptual part, Part 2, came from the practical part of me that wanted to share the fundamentals of organic gardening I have learned through education and experience. The second conceptual part, Part 3, is designed to encourage the reader to plant their own garden and consider the value that they personally can offer the natural world. It is meant as an introduction to not only an organic way of gardening but to an organic way of thinking as well. I want the reader to come away with the feeling that not only are they an integral part of their ecosystem, but actually, they are irreplaceable and highly valued.

In Part 1 Chapter 1, I simply tell my own story in an abbreviated format in order to set the scene. I talk about where and how I grew up and the trajectory my life took that compelled me to want to write a book about gardening in the first place. Beyond that, I attempt to introduce my own view of the natural world and how we gardeners can influence our surroundings to enhance our own lives as well as all the lives that exist within our local environment.

Chapter 2 is about tillage, or the lack thereof, because, in my personal gardening journey, removing tillage from my system is the single most revolutionary move I have made. In my opinion, *no-till*—also known as *no-dig*—methods of gardening are the foundation of a healthy organic food production system. Of course, you do not need to be farming organically to benefit from no-till; the fruits of that labor are for anybody interested in producing more from their land while using less input.

In the next chapter, I talk about soil. Soil, being the literal foundation of all life on Earth, should really come sooner, but I chose to start with the rototiller for chronological reasons due to the limitations of the human perspective. The simple truth is that you cannot even begin to build your soil until you forget about the rototiller. Once the natural process of organic matter covering the soil and decomposing slowly into the lower horizons[1] is established, living organisms return and, in time, bring balance back to an ecosystem. This kind of system lays the groundwork for a healthy garden and a healthy environment.

Chapter 4 is my personal favorite because it sums up my own view of the role of a gardener. Among many other things, I have always been a fan of *The Lord of the Rings,* and ever since I was little, I have had an obsession with the Ents, walking, talking trees that call themselves the "Shepherds of the Forest." This is how I try to view myself as I act in the garden because that garden does not actually end at my fence; it continues beyond borders, all around the world. What I do to promote health in my own little environment has ripples that spread out beyond comprehension. I try not to think of myself as an owner of plants. Instead, I use words like *friend, caretaker,* and maybe even *guardian,* but I always remember that each and every organism in my landscape belongs to

---

1   Horizons—Geologically distinct levels within undisturbed soil which develop over time and change with depth.

itself. I simply take care of their day-to-day needs, and in return, they nourish me and my family.

Chapter 5 is less scientific and more speculative. I am very interested in people's relationship with plants. I believe it is healthy to cultivate a personal relationship with nature and, more specifically, with the individual plants that nourish us with food, medicine, and clean air. This concept is given to the reader in hopes that they will bring that consideration with them into their gardening practice as well as their life more broadly speaking.

The following pages are accurate to the best of my ability and are always honest. I always try to maintain a sense of awe at the daily wonders of the world, whether I am reading, writing, hiking, speaking, or otherwise expressing myself. It is the little things in life that bring us the most pleasure. The smallest of interactions can just light up your life if you pay attention. So, as you go forward with the reading of this book and with your life in general, please stay curious and enjoy.

PART 1

Setting the Scene

'Tis in ourselves that we are thus or thus. Our bodies are our gardens, to the which our wills are gardeners.

—**William Shakespeare**

Throughout this book, I of course use the term *gardener* in the literal sense to describe someone who cultivates a garden. But also, often simultaneously, I will use it in a metaphorical sense as a means of alluding to someone who cultivates the lives around them so they might bear fruit.

CHAPTER 1.

What is a Gardener?

What is a gardener?

We are all gardeners, whether we realize it or not. For better or for worse, we all cultivate our own lives, and consciously or unconsciously, we cultivate the lives around us. Becoming aware of this interplay can be beneficial to us and the greater ecosystems we take part in. What is a gardener? I believe that you are a gardener. I myself am also a gardener, so to give you some perspective, I will tell you—in an abbreviated format—my own story.

I was born and raised in the heart of Mendocino County, California. My mother is from the Bay Area where her father worked as a landscaper. My father is from South Dakota, where just about everyone was a farmer. My dad has a Bachelor of Arts in environmental science; he received it back in the day, when such studies were considered an art rather than a hard science. He and my mother bought a house on the edge of a greenbelt[2], where they raised us kids on as much homegrown food as was possible in a shady location like Brooktrails.

As a result of this upbringing, I always had an appreciation for the natural world and a special love for fresh food. After high school, I wanted to go to Humboldt State University—now Cal-Poly Humboldt— so, having been accepted through instant admissions, I got a summer job working for my best friend's dad's landscaping business, just to save money. While working there, I began to feel a calling. Spending my days getting paid to breathe fresh air and exercise in the midst of beautifully landscaped gardens was like a dream come true. It was like waking up to the sound of a song playing in the distance. However, since my own dad was a gardener and I was of the age of rebellion, I resisted the calling. For the time being anyway. I took off to college and found myself taking religious studies and philosophy classes. My innate curiosity about the nature of the world is what drew me to such studies, and I learned a great number of life skills and beneficial belief systems while I was there. The ancient mystic traditions have a powerful hold on me, and I am sure that that may become apparent as you read this book. But still, as I

---

2   Greenbelt—Accessible public land that is protected through legal action from future development.

wandered the campus, I found myself obsessing over the landscapes present there too. I would fantasize about how I would plant my own garden if I had one. I would daydream about my favorite plants while I walked in the local community forest, all while still resisting the calling because I did not want to be like my dad. Such a childish thing to do, but still, eventually, my destiny caught up with me. As you will see.

After spending a year at HSU and loving every minute of it, I realized that I was not making enough money to pay for housing there, but I did not want to abandon my studies to work full-time yet. In the meantime, my older brother had moved back in with our parents and was playing soccer at the local community college with one of our mutual friends. After some debate, the two of them convinced me to come home and join them on the team. Living with my parents again was not ideal, but they helped me build a military-style tent on the property where I could have some space for myself. I was already losing interest in classroom learning, so having half of my semester units made up of outdoor activity would have been a plus even if soccer was not my favorite sport, which it was (and still is). But I was still not satisfied. There was something inside me just waiting to be released. A passion waiting to be awakened. Still just slightly out of tune. My life lacked harmony.

My first semester at Mendocino College, I had signed up for one online class thinking it would be easier than a physical one. My very first day, I was brutally disabused of such a notion. Being somewhat technologically challenged, I was completely overwhelmed by the amount of computer work that was assigned. See, I still had not become consciously aware of the dictates of my physiology or my body's unspoken need to express itself outdoors. You might even say I felt out of harmony. So I dropped the class and followed the invisible threads of destiny.

The problem I was left with was that, in order to play soccer, I had to be enrolled full-time in twelve units, so the search for a replacement class began. Flipping through the semester catalog, I happened across a class called Plant Identification, and a distant memory surfaced. The memory was of going on walks in the woods with my father as a kid and listening to him describe the Latin names for all the plants growing along the side of the path and their potential uses if they had any. My interest peaked, and the need for more units drove me on. I decided to sit in on the class and make up my mind afterwards. Needless to say, the teacher was great (he himself was a graduate from HSU, a university I will always love). He had an obvious passion for the study of the natural world, a passion that was contagious. So I got him to sign my paperwork, and I joined the class. The thing that had been sleeping in my subconscious was now awakened and only needed to be nurtured and raised. It needed to be cultivated.

Plant Identification was the best introduction for me because it was predominantly spent outside of the classroom and gave me a vocabulary to describe the landscapes I had already been subconsciously drawn to. I did not have a car, so I rode the bus forty-five minutes each way every day just to get to school. The lack of time and transportation made getting a job difficult, but the need for money drove me to innovate. I started to work in the Agriculture Department as a student worker taking care of nursery production and the two-acre demonstration gardens on campus. I probably learned as much on the job as I did in the classroom. The hands-on experience was irreplaceable. After a couple of years, I earned an associates degree in agriculture-horticulture, a certification in water-efficient landscaping, and a full-time job as nursery specialist at a local vineyard and olive farm that started as a simple internship. On top of all that lucky happenstance, I met my wife, Serena, in the Mendocino College Agriculture Department, so ultimately, I got an education, a job, and a family out of the deal. For all that, I am beyond grateful.

Serena became pregnant with our son during my last semester, which helped motivate me to find a full-time job. The internship opportunity came along shortly, providing a solution. The deal was, I would work a couple days a week until I graduated, and then I would come on board full-time after that. The job was a dream come true. I had the freedom to grow whatever I wanted to. For me, it was a lot of fun to take care of nursery production and vegetable production as well as the groundskeeping for the tasting room. On top of those duties, I was on call to help with bottling in the factory and caring for the various farm animals as needed. There, I really settled into the gardener persona and finally let go of any childish restraints I had surrounding my self-image. For just a little while, I found myself feeling like I was on top of the world, and I wondered where I could even go from there.

Then, one June day, I was on the job, driving stakes into the ground to tie up my tomato plants, a seemingly benign task, when I accidentally dropped a forty-pound post driver on my own head. The consequences of that injury have not left me yet, and I am beginning to accept that they might never. I suffered brain damage and spinal cord damage, resulting in more symptoms than I can remember, let alone write about, and more pain than I thought possible. I stopped working and spent the next couple of years recovering, raising my two young children—we had a daughter almost two years after the accident—thinking about my place in the world, and, of course, gardening in my home plot while my wife went back to work. My ability to work in the garden was dramatically affected by the injury, and still, years later, I have not recovered my old vigor. But the experience helped me to hone and solidify my views. I was forced to take a more relaxed approach than I used to, an approach that I try to relate to the reader in this writing. I was blessed with the lesson of forced attention. I learned the value of simple pleasures as a distraction from the ever-present despairs of life. I learned to create distance from my pain by focusing on caring for others beyond myself.

As I struggled with my health problems, I resorted to a very strict diet. Nowadays, I try my best to buy only organic produce. I avoid processed foods entirely, including sugar and wheat, and eat as much homegrown vegetables as I can manage. I feel a lot better doing so. "You are what you eat," after all. This is not a diet book, and I am not a dietitian, so I will not spend much time here, but I made those changes for a simple reason that is motivated by three more complicated concepts. The reason being that I feel better doing so. The motivation is as follows: Firstly, and most simply, I believe that the less distance from the farm to your stomach, the more nutrient-dense your food is. Secondly, I believe that, if you are happier about how your food is produced, you are more likely to digest that food smoothly. Thirdly, and most abstractly, I think that plants actually evolved alongside animals in order to produce certain "medicines" for the animals nearby, so it would logically follow that plants growing in your garden, especially if they have been there for multiple generations, will be better adapted to heal what ails you personally.

Being unemployed and mostly disabled has caused me to struggle with my identity and the value that I can offer the world. Wanting to still maintain a foothold in the world of agriculture I felt I had just entered, I made an Instagram account, aidens_gardening, and joined the Monarch Fellowship so I could grow and distribute milkweed—the host plant for Monarch butterflies—to my community in a grassroots conservation effort. I even opened my own native plants nursery, Madrone Wilds, which flopped before I was able to make a single sale. As soon as I had my license to sell plants at the Mendocino County farmers market, my wife and I bought a house we could afford in the neighboring county of Lake. My new permit was not valid for that county, but my family had a home, a beautiful home at that. I now had a well for water and a quarter acre of land to cultivate and experiment on. But I was still struggling with insecurity. I felt like I had all this knowledge gained through hard work, and yet I could not use it to serve my community. Any time that I struggled with these negative thoughts, I would find peace in my garden. This was my local community, the one I could always find a way to serve.

Then, one day, I had a talk with a good friend of mine about philosophy and gardening, two topics that do not always come up in the same conversation. Unless, of course, you are talking to me. He surprised me by suggesting that I write a book. It seemed like a good idea, so this is my attempt at that.

At the time of publishing this, I have finally been cleared by my doctor to go back to work—with some restrictions—and have happily taken up a job at the local Department of Agriculture and Weights and Measures as an insect trapper. My summer days are spent peacefully inspecting the beautiful vineyards of Lake County, California for pests. Summer nights are still spent in my own backyard. Cultivating. Harmonizing with my local community. Bonding with the garden.

"What is a garden?" you might ask.

A garden is a place where many diverse lives come together in harmony to create something beautiful. Harmony, we all know, is a song. We all have a frequency, a rhythm; we all have our own song. Your heart beats to the sound of nature. Plants' circulatory systems follow a natural rhythm as well. All these frequencies overlap and integrate. Similar frequencies strengthen each other, and others compete. We should seek to be in harmony with nature. We should spend our lives making music with our actions.

What is a gardener? What is a garden?

I hope to answer these questions, at least in part, within the pages of this book. In short, I believe that the whole world is a garden. An Eden. We are all just responsible for our own little piece of paradise.

Seeding the Soil: the Roots of the Matter

Avoiding soil disturbance is key, as it allows the natural processes within the soil to work without interference.

—*Charles Dowding*

Soil is more complicated than can be comprehended. Imposing human forcefulness on natural processes is unnecessary. It is hubris.

CHAPTER 2.

The Rototiller

When my siblings and I were little, our father's friend let us grow a vegetable garden on the lower part of his property. There was a small, seasonal pond on the shaded southwest side of the large clearing where the garden was. My dad put up deer fencing in the clearing to protect the veggies. When there was water in the pond, red-bellied newts could be seen swimming in it. When it was dry, you could see cracked mud patties that had formed on the bottom when the pond shriveled up. There was also a dry creek bed nearby, with colorful rocks and gnarly oak trees, and across the clearing from the pond were the neighbors, a very friendly elderly couple who owned a couple of noisy guinea hens. For kids like my big brother, my little sister, and myself, it was a kind of paradise. A place for wonder, mystery, adventure, and just plain old fun.

It was at first anyway.

The first time we went up there was the most exciting as well as the most disappointing. We kids took to our new playground like a dog to a bone. Pretty soon, however, the sun was beating down, and I was already burned, scraped, and dusty from playing in the creekbed. This is when my dad called us over to help work in the garden. That is what we were there to do, after all. The first thing he had us do was walk along behind him as he rototilled and picked up all the rocks, which we put in a pile just outside the deer fence. It was amazing to me how, no matter how many rocks I removed, there were always more when I came back. This was especially impressive when we came back consecutive years and there were still more rocks to be found in that one little plot of land. Watching that machine go to work breaking up the earth in preparation for our planting was exhilarating, and to this day, I think I would still get a thrill out of running a rototiller even though I use a different system now and do not support tillage as a general rule.

This is, I believe, something men struggle with more than women, generally speaking. We enjoy aggressive or destructive actions—which is necessary at times, more so in other parts of history than now probably—but the patterns in our nervous systems are difficult to shake. I also enjoy weed eating, even though the conservationist in me thinks there might be a better way. It is fun to cut grass. And it is fun to break ground. It is fun to rototill.

When I was twenty-one, I worked at a CCOF certified organic winery and olive mill. The owners of this place are very conscientious farmers, and one of them, a seasoned Swiss farmer, came up to me while I was tilling in preparation for a landscape planting—something I would never do now—and said, "The rototiller is the earthquake that destroyed the city."

I had already had other teachers that spoke of the benefits of no-till farming, but this statement finally struck home with me. All the lifeforms that exist within the soil beyond just the weeds, which were all I really wanted to remove, were also being removed. Everything from earthworms to fungi were having their entire world turned upside down—literally—and I had never stopped to consider their well-being before. The analogy of a city being destroyed by an earthquake was just vivid enough an image to finally get through to me. With that statement, the seed had been planted in my mind, but it still took some time to grow. It still took me some time to break away from that destructive habit.

That same year, I was the main person responsible for the vegetable garden at said winery, and I had been debating with myself on whether or not I should till before planting. Not only was I becoming skeptical of the actual benefit, but it was also a hassle. We did not own a small enough tiller for the vegetable plot, and it was too awkward to get the tractor in without the risk of running over irrigation equipment anyway. So we would have to rent one. It all seemed like an unnecessary headache when we had good soil structure and quality manure sources on the farm already, but when I brought it up to my superior—not the previously mentioned owner but one of the guys who actually ran operations—he said, "Of course we are going to till. We always do." And we did. Naturally, that is how such things tend to play out. Tradition wins.

The main problem with tillage is it disrupts the natural processes that occur in healthy soil. It breaks roots, both dead and alive, all while mixing organic mulch with topsoil, speeding up decomposition, releasing carbon (and other gasses) into the air, wasting nutrients, and compacting the deeper horizons of soil even more. These actions dissect, desiccate, and suffocate soil organisms. Organisms which are necessary for the production of biological compounds that, in sufficient amounts, generate healthy soil structure and cause the release of vital plant nutrients which can be locked up in mineral forms.

The reason many farmers use tillage is because it eases the process of planting, and by speeding up the decomposition of organic matter, more nutrients are made available to the plants. The problem there is that plants did not evolve to grow in monocrops on tilled soil. They evolved in diverse communities teaming with a variety of other organisms and have developed important relationships with many of them. When you till, you harm these other organisms which harms their relationship, a relationship founded on support. Plants who form mycorrhizal associations with mushrooms can survive with less water, have access to more nutrients, and have stronger immune systems than solitary plants. There are also bacteria in the soil which capture nitrogen from the air and make it available to plants as well as bacteria and algae that produce oxygen, a necessary chemical for healthy root function. All of these beneficial organisms are harmed by the rototiller. A farmer might argue that it is worth it because they can make more nutrients available to the plant quicker with tillage, but I would argue that the plant cannot actually access all that nutrition all at once. This is why so much valuable plant food is lost into the air or in runoff from conventional farming operations. This results in more fertilizer being tilled in next season just to be washed away again.

Come back next year and do it again. Spend a fortune at the ag supply store, fire up the rototiller, and get to work picking up rocks like it is the first time again.

Rinse and repeat.

Or you could build a system and seek to grow life in your garden, not crops. Layer organic matter on top of the soil and let natural processes take charge of fertilizing when the time is right. All you need to do is make sure that there is fertility available in the form of organic mulch on top of the soil. The worms, arthropods, and microorganisms will take care of mixing it for you without damaging roots or the soil structure. This kind of approach does not give the grower as much of a sense of control and does not always yield as much immediately, but in the long run, it tends to improve yield year after year, all while costing a fraction as much money to maintain.

"But what about loosening the soil?" you might ask. "Is it not beneficial for roots to grow in broken ground?" The simple truth that blew my mind when I first learned it is that the growth tip of a plant's root exudes far greater pressure than the tines of a rototiller is even capable of. This means that there is no ground your tiller can break through that a root cannot. The rototiller does not give plants access to more soil; in fact, it only drives compaction deeper into the soil. If you want to have a fluffy aerated growth medium, just mulch with an abundance of organic material and build higher, looser horizons without damaging or distorting lower ones. When making new beds, you can lay cardboard on top of the ground before mulching to help smother weeds. This actually works much more effectively than rototilling.

For more information on no-till methods, you can check the resources listed at the end of the book.They are just some of the places I find myself revisiting in search of ever more practical information. There are other places to learn about such things of course, but as I will reiterate throughout this book, there is no substitute for personal experience. If you are thinking about planting a garden, go ahead and put this book down—for now—and head on down to your local nursery or hardware store. Pick up a pack of seeds or a potted plant and place them in some untilled earth. It is just that easy to get started.

Seeding the Soil: the Roots of the Matter

The organicist is the scientist of this new agriculture and his garden is his laboratory.

—Gene Longsdon

To call organic agriculture new is almost laughable, even back in the seventies when this quote was published, but still, it rings true that you can—and should—make important scientific discoveries in your own backyard.

CHAPTER 3.
The Dirt (Soil)

Now we get into the dirty details about what really makes the garden grow.

The dirt.

My horticulture teacher in the Mendocino College Agriculture Department, Jim Xerogenis, used to say—and I believe he was quoting one of his own teachers when he did—"Dirt is what's under your fingernails; soil is what plants need."

But what is the difference?

Soil is alive and full of nutrition.

Dirt is just dirty. Dust for the dustpan.

When your vegetables get the nutrition they need, so do you. Plants have physical signs that signify when

29

they are getting all the micro- and macronutrients that they need. Some of these signs are increased branching or budding, larger leaves with more leaflets, early or especially vigorous blooming, and increased pubescens (fuzziness) on leaves and young stems. Other more noticeable signs of a healthy plant are strong scents and flavors. Melons are sweeter, peppers are hotter, and herbs are more pungent when grown in soils that are prepared to provide all the nutrients needed for the optimal health of the plants in question.

Most gardeners are aware that plants require three main nutrients for growth: nitrogen, phosphorus, and potassium, commonly referred to as N, P, and K. As seen in *Botany for Gardeners,* there are eight other basic macronutrients required for plant growth: carbon (C), hydrogen (H), oxygen (O), sulfur (S), calcium (Ca). In addition, there are seven more, somewhat misleadingly labeled *micronutrients.* I say this is misleading because they are called micronutrients due to being required in smaller concentrations than the macronutrients, not because they are actually inferior or unnecessary. The truth is, all fourteen nutrients are absolutely necessary for plant life, so they should all be taken into consideration. The seven listed as micronutrients by Brian Capon in *Botany for Gardeners* are magnesium (Mg), manganese (Mn), iron (Fe), copper (Cu), zinc (Zn), boron (B), and molybdenum (Mu). Many people claim that the first three of these—N, P, and K—are the main macronutrients, listing all others as "micronutrients" because the macros are still needed in higher quantities than the others and are very important for growing healthy crops. But as I said before, they are all indispensable, so there is little reason for me to argue either way about how to categorize them. As long as they are all present, I am happy. No gardening book would be complete without mentioning these nutrients, but my approach to plant nutrition is more relaxed than conventional. So, if you are going to forget anything from this book, make it the nonsense I just said that sounds like variables in an algebra problem. Gardening is supposed to be fun, after all, not stressful. So long as you continue to add organic matter sourced from living organisms to your soil, you will have all the nutrients needed to support more life. For that reason, very little attention is paid in this book to specific nutrients. Instead, the emphasis is placed on enhancing life in the soil in general. Life breeds more life, after all.

The best way to add more life to your soil in the form of organic matter and make sure it has all the nutrients your plants need, is to fertilize (topdress) with finished compost that was made with a diversity of different organic materials. The best way to ensure the contents of your compost is to make it yourself. If materials, time, or energy are an issue, you can also always find a local source for compost and ask them about their process and what goes into making their product. I want to emphasize this point because, if you are going to purchase compost, it is best if it is made locally.

There are countless ways to make compost at home, and there are much better resources than myself for that kind of information. I will get into the basics here, but if you want more detail, look elsewhere, and I might also suggest that you start making some compost for yourself because there is no better teacher than hands-on experience. It is not the last time you will hear me say this, so get used to it. Anyone can give it a try.

To start with, compost is simply decomposed organic matter that can be used to amend garden soil. Any pile of organic matter, if left to its own devices, will eventually break down into humus, which is the main active component of compost sought after by agriculturalists. Humus is far from a simple substance because it teems with biological potential, but to the naked eye, it just appears to be soft black or brown soil that vaguely resembles finely ground coffee. If you are patient, you can just pile all your garden and kitchen waste in one place and let it break down on its own. Turning the pile occasionally is beneficial but not necessary. Ideally, you want to maintain an aerated structure so that the pile does not get anaerobic; you will know if it does because it will develop a nasty smell. While being careful not to submerge the air pockets, you still want to maintain a constant moisture level whenever possible. Slow compost like this provides an ideal habitat for earthworms, which will hasten decomposition and enhance the quality of your finished product. To encourage worms, build layers of different materials into your pile and turn it carefully.

If you do these things, you can have some usable compost ready in about six months to a year.

If you want your compost in a hurry, you need to be prepared for a little more work. If you utilize this hot composting method, you can have finished humus quite quickly. It is referred to as *hot compost* because the increased number of microorganisms present creates an impressive amount of body heat. For this reason, you do have to be more strict about turning and moistening your pile, and you should also be more selective about what you put into it. The smaller materials are when they go in, the faster they decompose. That being said, having objects of diverse sizes in the pile improves porosity and aeration. You also have to be more aware of your carbon (browns) to nitrogen (greens) ratio. High carbon materials are things like wood chips and rice hulls, which take longer than high nitrogen materials to break down. Your nitrogen materials are things like green leaves, fresh grass clippings, and most kitchen scraps. You can also up your nitrogen with organic fertilizers like fish emulsion or feather meal. Just read the packaging for information on nitrogen content. Different books will recommend different amounts of these different materials, but most of them require previous knowledge of the chemical composition of each material and an unnecessary amount of math. What I will tell you to do is what I do myself. I just try to keep things as diverse as possible. You can use the eyeball method. Visually, you want roughly half greens and half browns, with things cut up into a variety of different sizes and mixed thoroughly to create a fluffy structure. Both cold compost—described above—and hot compost—the currently depicted method—piles function best when they are at least three square feet in size. The larger your pile, the faster it will decompose. If you make compost this way, you can expect it to be ready every two to eight weeks in the summer and every one to six months in the colder months.

Personally, I have made both hot and cold compost and used lots of different kinds of materials to do so. My favorite kind of compost for the vegetable garden is cold vermicompost[3] because it is teaming with micro- and macroorganisms whose lives enrich the soil and most closely emulate the ecosystem you want to support. The goal is a soil that is aerobic and dominated by fungus, with healthy soil aggregates held together by a diversity of organic substances. My favorite materials to make compost with are a combination of brown leaves (45%), green leaves (20%), brown stalks like corn or sunflower (5%), fresh and/or aged manure (20%), and small kitchen scraps (10%).

These percentages are estimates and are only included to give the reader a ballpark recommendation. Using whatever materials are easily available to you is always recommended. That being said, I would like to include more specific suggestions for the more serious reader or

---

3   Vermicompost: Compost produced through the digestive actions of earthworms.

anyone with more resources available. First, I want to highlight the guideline, mentioned above, to only use small kitchen scraps, preferably shredded, because these tend to be high in water and can cause anaerobic pockets in the pile. It is also generally recommended that you do not put meat or other oily foods in the compost because they will also make wet spots and can invite scavengers, like racoons, to root around in your pile. If you are seeking nutrient-rich compost, use more manure and select for better quality manure. When you are using it as a mulch, manure should be well-aged, but when adding it to the compost pile, you want it to be as fresh as you can get it. Fresh manure has much higher nutrient content than aged manure, and in addition to that, different animals excrete different qualities of manure. Chicken manure is very high in all three macronutrients and very easy to acquire. Mammal manure is lower in nutrient than poultry manure but breaks down better in a pile and can be added in larger amounts. Horse manure has better structure than cow manure and is less likely to become anaerobic, but it tends to come with weed seeds, whereas the complex stomachs of grazing cattle easily break such seeds down during digestion. Sheep and goat droppings are one of my favorites to work with, but they are more difficult to collect because they come in pellets rather than patties and these are not as easily scooped up.

The most convenient kind of manure for most gardeners is one that is commonly overlooked. Insect droppings are not only easily accessible to most gardeners, but they are also surprisingly nutrient-dense, boost plants' immune systems, and are naturally abundant when conditions are right. If you create a habitat for them, insects will spend more time doing what they do and doing doo-doo in your garden. If you feel like it, you can build a container and farm earthworms or mealybugs or any other insect you find interesting. Then, spread their castings in the garden. The simplest way, however, is to just create a habitat that encourages a diversity of resident insects. To do this, plant densely with a variety of different species. Ensure that the soil is always covered with plants or organic matter such as wood chips or straw and that there are flowers in bloom all year round. These simple things make a world of difference to our little neighbors. If you build it, they will come.

Composting and insect farming are great practices for the home and market gardens, but the best way to incorporate manure into a full-scale farm is to include these livestock in your system and rotate them on the land, allowing the natural order of things to take place. In addition to grazing livestock, there is immeasurable value in growing cover crops. There should never be bare soil in a growing space. The need some farmers have to let fields go fallow[4] is a sign of a systemic issue. Their systems do not allow for enough diversity to buffer

---

4   Fallow—Agricultural practice where planting zones are intentionally left bare of plants in order to recover from pest or disease issues in those particular zones.

against invasion and infection in the monocrop. You do not have to buy a cover crop seed mix, though there can be an added benefit; you can just be more relaxed about your weeding. Avoid spraying herbicides. Pull out obnoxious plants like bindweed and Bermuda grass when they get in your way but allow things like purslane, yarrow, dandelion, and plantain to grow freely in unused space. Plants like these, which are often unkindly referred to as "weeds," provide a number of benefits. Many of them are edible or medicinal. All of them maintain a healthy structure within the soil and sustain diverse communities of microorganisms through the excretion of energy-rich root exudates. Just like any gardener, I have many favorite plants and also a list of plants to avoid, but that being said, I believe that *any* plant is a *good* plant if the alternative is no plants at all. All plants photosynthesize, creating biologically accessible energy from the sun, fulfilling their roles as primary producers, and providing the necessary foundation for all life to exist on Earth. This should not be taken for granted.

If there is anything I have learned from talking to lots of different gardeners—a practice I suggest for anyone who considers *themselves* to be a gardener—it is that everyone—and I mean everyone—has a different system. So the best way to find out what your system is is to just jump right in. Play with different things and find out what works for you and your location's unique conditions. As long as the basic natural processes are allowed just as they would be in a forest, your soil will be a solid foundation for life to take hold. Minimize soil disturbance and keep healthy green plants covering its surface. Beyond that, the artistry is up to you, the gardener.

Feeding the Soul: the Fruits and the Labor

We have reached a critical period. The harm done by the widespread use of poisons is becoming increasingly apparent and grave. . . . Yet modern science, which has given us the chemical pesticides, has also given us deeper insights into basic biological laws that govern all living organisms.

—Beatrice Trum Hunter

A statement made fifty years ago that has only become more accurate, more relevant, and simply more true as time has passed, yet for me, it is an encouraging look at the potential future state of agriculture rather than a discouraging warning. Change takes time, but it is always inevitable.

CHAPTER 4.

A System, Not a Crop

I like worms in my garden. My son—aged two years old at the time of writing this—likes digging worms up from the garden. Initially, I wanted to curb that behavior, but the truth is, as a resident here, he is as much a part of the garden himself as the worms or even the crops. I had to find a way to integrate his tendencies and use them to promote life in the garden rather than hinder it. So I taught him to dig up worms and carry them to the compost pile, where they would be safely deposited. We made a game of it. He got excited and managed that chore just fine.

The goal is to see the garden as a system, not a crop. You are responsible for the well-being of every lifeform present in the space you are cultivating. Leave a weed in the ground, and you feed the insects a plant that you are not going to eat. Then, in turn, the insects will feed the birds so they will not be interested in eating your vegetables. In this way, you turn a potential pest into a pesticide, turn a predator upon another predator, and, in doing so, establish balance in the ecosystem. This kind of approach only works when you treat the garden as a system, not as a crop. You have to consider the potential value of every plant, insect, fungus, bacteria, rodent, and bird within your space and try to develop a niche for them where they can live comfortably without disrupting the other organisms in the system.

At my home, I am working on creating a native flower garden alongside my vegetable garden that will provide a habitat and food source for insects that will benefit the system I want to facilitate. In this garden, I planted a Cleveland sage, which is a very fast-growing California native that the bumblebees love. Underneath this sage is a massive colony of Argentine ants. Argentine ants are the ones with a black head and butt and a red body, and they are a well-known agricultural pest because they farm aphids, scales, and other soft-bodied insects who feed on the sap of growing plants. These particular ants had colonized my Cleveland sage with an abundance of black aphids, moving them around to the healthiest parts of the plant to suck sap and excrete honeydew (poop), which the ants then harvested in order to feed their own growing colony under the ground.

When I first noticed this abundance of pests in the garden, I got worried and, like most gardeners would, considered spraying them with soap, which can be used to kill soft-bodied insects, including aphids and ants. But I reminded myself that this is the exact reason I wanted to plant native perennials next to my vegetable crops: so that I could provide food for the insects that live in my community and, in doing so, try to close the loop and complete the system. So I held off on the soapy insecticide and just watched what happened. The first thing I noticed was the fact that the Cleveland sage was by far the happiest and healthiest plant in the garden at the time, and so it was no wonder that the ants had chosen it as their host. It was the plant that was producing enough energy not only to thrive on its own but to provide an entire city of aphids and a colony of ants with all the food they needed without even batting an eye. The plant is healthy, the aphids are healthy, the ants are healthy, and I have not noticed a single black aphid on any of my other plants (the "crops"). On top of that happy ending, I know that I am also allowing a steady source of food for well-known garden friends like ladybugs and green lacewings, who love to snack on aphids. This means I will be able to maintain a population of beneficial insects so that, when the pests do choose to invade the vegetable garden, I know there will be defenders already in place to keep the balance.

In fact, only a couple of months passed before I noticed several hungry ladybugs feasting on the Aphid

Buffet. Just by planting one native Salvia[5], I was able to feed an entire ecosystem of insects, and all this happened before the plant even made any flowers to feed the bees, butterflies, and hummingbirds or any seeds for the turkeys, doves, and field mice to eat. This single plant was able to improve the health of the entire ecosystem around it and, in doing so, indirectly improved the health of any crops I chose to grow nearby.

If you are having a problem with a pest, do not think, "This pest is a problem, and I need to eliminate it." Instead, think, "This problem is a sign of an imbalanced ecosystem," and then ask yourself, "What is missing that would restore balance?" For instance, if you are having problems with gophers or moles, I suggest you get a cat. If you are allergic or have another reason to not get a cat, you can build roosts in your garden for raptors like hawks and owls to perch on. You can use any kind of sturdy pipe to construct one of these. Make a T shape at the top of a single pipe or post to hold it up. These need to be tall, at least twenty feet high. Think about the average height of trees in your area, and that will be about how high your local raptors will prefer to hunt from. They need to be well-anchored as well, so take that into account. A resident cat is usually simpler, though, if you like bird watching, the perch might be worthwhile for that reason alone. If you are interested in attracting

5   Salvia—Latin name for plants in the Sage genus, referring, in this case, to the Cleveland sage.

birds to your yard—along with other wildlife—but you do not want to build such a structure, the best thing to do is to plant a native tree, like an oak or a willow.

Every different plant you choose to put in the garden will have a different effect on its surroundings, so you have to take into consideration the effect you want to have. That being said, do not be overly concerned about planting known host plants to pests you know are already present in the garden. For example, in my garden, I was always seeing white butterflies (cabbage loopers), which lay their eggs on brassicas (cabbage, brussels sprouts, broccoli, mustard, etc.). When the eggs hatch there, caterpillars can completely decimate a brassica crop. But I love growing brassicas for a variety of reasons. Their root exudates repel certain pests, they are productive in the cold months—here in California—and they taste delicious. So I planted some even though I knew the dreaded looper was nearby, and I waited, and I watched.

What I saw was a lot of adult butterflies in the garden, and I saw lots of their eggs on the leaves of my vegetables, but I never saw a single caterpillar, and I only saw very minimal damage to the plants. This was confusing to me at first, so I thought about what must be going on, and I watched some more. I figured that, with the numbers of eggs on my plants and the number of adults around, my plants should show more signs of damage. The wild mustard growing nearby could account for the number of adults flying in, but it did not explain why I never saw any in the larval form when there were clearly a lot of eggs being laid. As I puzzled over this, I noticed a lot of birds hanging around in the garden, and that is when it struck me—the birds must be eating all of the caterpillars. This was a relief because my initial knee-jerk reaction was to worry that the birds were after my cabbages too.

It just so happened that, again, by waiting and watching rather than reacting, I got another lesson in why you should treat your garden as a system and not as a single crop because you can always turn a potential problem into something that benefits the whole community. Your job as the gardener is just to guide each individual into the position that most benefits everybody.

I have found that companion planting is always a good idea, and contrary to common practice, it is actually beneficial to both annuals and perennials to grow them together. Perennials set roots down deep that draw up nutrients from below the reach of the annuals and reapply them to the surface as leaf litter. They can also provide protection from intense sun or frigid frost to annuals, which are more sensitive to such things. In return, annuals provide a living mulch that protects perennial roots from losing moisture during drought and increases porosity, allowing good drainage during flooded conditions.

Different kinds of plants have different light needs. To optimize light use in your garden in the northern hemisphere, you should plant the tallest things—generally fruit trees—on the northernmost end and progressively plant shorter and shorter ones as you move south. Since the sunlight comes in from the south, this allows the most light to reach the foliage of your crops. South of the equator, the reverse is true. Of course, this is a general guideline and not a rule. You might want to experiment with variations that allow for more diverse microclimates to form inside the garden. For example, some plants, like spinach and lettuce, prefer to grow in the shade during the summer. These plants I might tuck underneath a tree or shrub rather than take the time to construct an inorganic shade structure.

I have found that tubers and root vegetables can be grown in surprising proximity to other plants without disturbing each other because the majority of their growth is underground. They also lend themselves to the no-till garden because you can leave a few in the ground to resprout each year without fear of running them over with the cultivator. In my own garden, I have carrots, onions, and garlic naturalized, returning year after year to feed my family. I also know a lot of people who have permanent potato patches on their property because, even if they try to, they never manage to dig all of them up. So, in my own garden, I just make sure to leave a few of my favorite varieties at the end of the season to go to seed or divide underground. You do not have to limit this natural reseeding process to root vegetables either; I have just found that they are the most space-efficient, as plants generally take up more space when they are fruiting and making seeds.

Other plants that I like to grow from seed and save year after year are beans, peas, corn (if you have space), beets, melons, cilantro, and squash. If I am planning on saving seed, I always find an heirloom variety that me and/or my family prefer, and then I try to stick to growing just that one because cross-pollination can dilute the particular genetic traits we prefer. Then again, some plants benefit from diversity and will not even produce seed unless pollinated by multiple different parent plants, so it is always good to do research on any particular plant of interest, and I will reiterate—again, I know—there is no replacement for personal experimentation.

Every garden comes with unique problems, like my son with his worms, and every gardener has to come up with their own unique solutions. The point of this chapter is to offer a few examples and options for the budding gardener. Just remember that your garden is a system that integrates the lives of countless organisms and should not be reduced simply to the product your main crop produces.

Feeding the Soul: the Fruits and the Labor

The one who plants trees, knowing that he will never sit in their shade, has at least started to understand the meaning of life.

—Rabindranath Tagore

When you are able to see benefits from your own actions generations into the future and plan for the well-being of all beings on Earth, you will begin to grasp at the value that your own life offers the world.

CHAPTER 5

Personal Relations (Soul)

When I was very little, somewhere between the ages of five and ten, I can remember being heartbroken when my father cut down a few of the trees on the edge of our property to let more light into the garden. When he explained to me that the vegetables we eat needed more sun to grow, I understood his motivation, but I still complained because those particular trees had been my friends and I knew I would miss their presence any time I went playing in that part of the woods. And every day, when I looked out at the edge of the forest from the livingroom window to see their silhouettes permanently gone from the stand, my heart ached. To this day, into adulthood, I try to maintain that childlike affection for plants, not only for the ones that I cultivate but for all who share this beautiful planet with me.

I like to play in the garden. And I invite the plants to play with me. I attempt to blend conventional agricultural methods with natural biological processes. My landscaping reflects these concepts by combining organic plant forms with geometric rows and spacing. When designing a new garden, I imagine what it will look like from all directions—including from above. I picture what colors will bloom when and try to contrast various plant types with each other.

Think of a living tapestry.

A flowering mandala, cycling colors in rhythm with the seasons.

I was taught that a walk through the garden should engage all of the senses. You can taste and smell many plants along the way. You can feel the different textures of leaves or the crunch of gravel or dry leaf matter under your feet. As I just alluded to, a proper garden is also a feast for the eyes. Even the ears can be stimulated by birdsong or the gurgling of a water feature or the pleasant sound of a wind chime.

The beauty in the garden should mimic the beauty we see in the wild. We are born naturally into the natural world, all of us, and we live our best lives when we have positive relations with the land and life-forms that sustain us and bring joy into our lives.

However, these days, the common thread is that we have lost touch with nature, and I think that this is true in part but only in the sense that we are often unhappy because we do not spend enough time in beautiful places anymore and the greatest source of beauty is nature. But the idea that we are actually apart from nature and need to return to it is nonsense. Instead, we are a part of nature. An inseparable part. Cities are not the problem because we have always lived in communities like that for the sake of sharing resources. It makes the most sense for us to concentrate ourselves into these colonies for the sake of efficiency, but the way we design our cities can be and is being rethought. That is a topic for a whole other book, though. My point is that we humans are just a small part of a massive network of life-forms on this planet and each one plays a valuable role.

Your garden is a forest; it is an ecosystem governed by the same natural laws. Treat it as such.

When we humans settle in a new area, what do we do? We start, just like my father demonstrated, by cutting down the trees to let more light in because we need it to produce vitamin D and, more obviously, in order to grow food. Then, we mill the corpses of those trees and use them to build a comfy little home to raise our children in. Next, we introduce other new species to the area which are symbiotic and beneficial to us, like cows and chickens—and, of course, vegetables. In turn, these new species act on the surrounding environment to influence it in a direction that is more suitable to their lifestyles as well as our own. The cattle will eat up all of the slow-growing perennials and compact the land, turning it into pasture. This pasture is ideal for the cattle, but it also benefits us as bipedal hunters. We prefer open spaces where we can see for long distances. Chickens, similarly, turn up the soil when they eat, selecting for and spreading a variety of fast-growing weeds, which are a prime food source for them and, coincidentally, tend to be medicinal to us. Now that we are in a new area and have made things easier for predators by clearing the trees and introducing foreign livestock, we have to worry about protecting said livestock from predation. So we bring dogs. Dogs bring with them their own benefits and needs that are balanced by another introduction. And then come cats because the mice like prairie too and have eaten all our grain stores. You see, I could go on and on like this because it is not just humans that live in colonies and influence their environment to benefit the colony. All species act and interact in a manner that is intended to benefit them and their offspring (and the other species that benefit them and their offspring) including—or especially—plants. Considering that they cannot just get up and move like we can when conditions do not benefit them, plants are very invested in conditioning their surroundings to be more accommodating. Even more comfortable.

Our relationship with plants is codependent; I would even go so far as to say symbiotic. We inhale oxygen and exhale carbon dioxide. They inhale carbon dioxide and exhale oxygen. This is an ancient relationship that is so integral to our very existence that it is often overlooked and underappreciated. But does this codependence go deeper than that? Since I started to pay closer attention to my horticultural interests as well as my own health, I have begun to suspect that it does.

Plants that have existed in close proximity to humans for centuries have developed chemicals that fit perfectly into our neuroreceptors, indicating a deeper symbiosis. Plants not only feed and heal us but are also capable of eliciting experiences of awe and spiritual insight. All of our medicines are made from naturally occurring compounds, the majority of which are found in plants. Our own systems are designed as an intricate part of a much larger system. This larger system, which we can only begin to understand, has its own built-in immune system designed to protect its vital parts, just like our own.

We should want to befriend the plants that produce the air we breathe, the food we eat, and the medicine that heals us when we are sick. Through the simple process of respiration, we bond with plants on a molecular level, and it is happening all the time. I think we should want to spend as much time with the *same* plants as possible so that we can strengthen that bond and make it more personal. We all know that personal relationships are the healthiest; I think that actually goes without saying. When one is in the garden, they should be aware of the fact that this gentle, ever-present ebb and flow of breath that we take part in is nearly as ancient and powerful as the ebb and flow of the tides. As we breathe, the oxygen molecules produced inside of plants are absorbed into our own bodies to nourish and energize us. In turn, the carbon dioxide we release as waste is absorbed into the plants' bodies and used to create sugars that nourish and energize the plants. In the vegetable garden, that relationship can go another step further when the plants nourish you with sugars, starches, oils, and complex carbohydrates produced by them just for you out of appreciation for nurturing and cultivating them. By ensuring the health of your *environment,* you insure your *own* health—and yes, I say it like that because such a statement exceeds the realm of gardening to encompass all relationships.

I suspect that, if you spend your time cultivating plants that you and your family will eat, you will be healthier than if you buy equally nutritious food at the supermarket. It is only an instinct I have, and I have very little scientific evidence to prove it, but it makes sense to me that, if you spend an extended amount of time exchanging energy with *specific* living, breathing beings, you are going to have a healthier relationship with your personal source of energy. By having a healthier relationship with your energy source, you will feel a strong sense of pride as well as a relaxing sense of stability, self-sufficiency and interdependence. These senses are precursors to the feeling of awe, which I believe is an instinct designed to indicate when we are behaving appropriately for our nature. The more often we experience awe in our lives, the more likely we are to feel at peace or like we are living life appropriately. It is well-documented that spending time in nature improves mental health.

One of my favorite meditations is to think of my garden simply as a part or extension of the one and only garden that is planet Earth. When I do this, not only does it reinforce the value of how I manage my natural spaces naturally by highlighting the fact that my garden supports wildlife from beyond its borders, but it also reminds me when I am out and about in the world that I should treat all outdoor spaces with the same attention and care that I would my own home. Each and every plant and animal that is introduced to a new environment brings with it its very own microbiome and microclimate that support its own interests. There is no telling how far those ripples can go into the environment. When grown next to each other or in rotation, most plants are synergistic, and yet other combinations will shade, strangle, or even poison each other. But, again, in my experience, the majority of plants are complementary. In fact, plants are more like us humans than we generally realize.

All this intimate interplay indicates a kind of synergizing that happens between organisms in a shared environment. Plants and animals that harmonize together support each other's interests and, in doing so, generate an energy field that emanates into the surrounding area, drawing life with a similar vibration toward it and replicating it at a faster and faster rate. This speaks to the concept I introduced at the beginning of this book, the concept of a garden—or any other other natural space—resembling a song. One that we, as gardeners, can take part in. We can even become the lead singer if we do it right. Or something more like a symphony conductor.

In the interest of writing your own music on the earth, you should spend some time studying it. You might be surprised by what you see when you take the time to sit still and just observe the world around you.

One time, when I was lucky enough to be in such a present state of mind, I witnessed a raven doing something quite clever. He had collected a walnut from my neighbor's tree and was perched on the power lines above the road right in front of my house. From that vantage point, he was repeatedly dropping the nut down on the hard concrete until it cracked open, revealing the fleshy prize inside. I was initially surprised by the bird's ingenuity, but in retrospect, I should have expected such intelligence from any of Earth's many creatures. We are all experts in our own field. Uniquely designed to fit a niche environment on this diverse planet. Unfortunately, I suffer, like all humans, from an intellectual hubris. You do not have to be intellectual to be intelligent. That is one of the lessons I have learned by observing nature closely.

Gardeners often get heckled for personifying the plants in their gardens. The same can be said for pet owners who use fake voices to express their dog's emotions that cannot otherwise be communicated and, in doing so, invent an anthropomorphic personality. We often make light of this as if it is just a joke, but the truth is that all living organisms on this planet have similar behaviors and thought patterns. We are all more like each other than we are different. It is just the differences that stand out. Maybe it is not inappropriate to talk to your plants or to talk for your dogs; maybe you really do understand them that well. Or maybe I am just trying to justify my own personality traits, seeing as I fall into both of these categories. It is hard to say, but I think the evidence is leaning in my favor.

The key point I am trying to make is that the gardener is not just the cultivator or the product manager; they are a very unique part of the garden. They get to be the puppet master and the audience. The one who acts and the one who watches the results of said actions like a cosmic play.

Just recently, I went out into the garden to check on my Turkish cliff sage (Salvia recognita) because it was blooming and I thought I had seen a bee on it from inside my living room. I went out the sliding glass window and walked across the backyard to get a closer look. This particular sage has little pink flowers like puckered lips that blow kisses to the pollinators it is attracting. It is planted right next to my pomegranate tree close to the back fence. Sure enough, when I got there, I saw a big black carpenter bee happily buzzing around, feeding on the flowers, a light dusting of pollen coating its head. I had watched this bumblebee for about a minute as it hummed around from one little nectar source to another when, suddenly, an additional carpenter bee—with an even heavier pollen dusting—came zooming in out of nowhere and attacked the first bee. They wrestled around for a little while, bumping into the surrounding foliage, and then the first bee flew off and did not come back. The new bee, with his heavy pollen dusting, then jealously stood guard, buzzing in circles around the pink blossoms, occasionally stopping in midair to look left and then right before buzzing around again in a patrol and, likely, a show of dominance. It was interesting to see such sophisticated behavior from a simple insect, patrolling and defending a favored food source from the competition. I should note that, throughout this whole interaction, I, the observer and innocent bystander, was less than a foot from the plant and the quarrelsome insects, and they never bothered with me since I was not seen as a threat in their world and possibly was not even seen at all. All the while, I knew that the flowers they were fighting over so intensely were flowers I had planted there myself with the intention of attracting such pollinators to the garden.

As you get more in tune with your local environment, another thing you will start to notice is patterns that repeat as the seasons change. For instance, I have noticed that, in my own area, the flowers bloom in sequence with each other. First come the blue and the purple flowers early in the spring. Then, later on, in unison, come the yellows and the oranges. Summer brings on the red blooms and more oranges. When fall starts to turn into winter, I see predominately white flowers in bloom.

I have a theory as to why this happens. The botanical community knows that plants tend to prefer different pollinators or, in reality, that different pollinators prefer different types of plants. It is likely that insects see in various different colors, so some are easier for them to see than others. An insect's life cycle is fairly short too, and most bees are only capable of flying during specific temperature ranges, so the pollinators that are active in a garden will vary depending on the time of day as well as the seasons. I think that bees who prefer cooler-colored flowers, like blues and violets, are the first ones to come out in the spring around here. Then come those who prefer warmer colors, like yellow, orange, and, eventually, red. I think that the white flowering plants are more heavily represented in the winter months because white flowers are easier to see at night, making them favored by nocturnal insects, such as moths. Winter nights are longer, allowing for an extended period of pollinator activity.

If you practice being conscious in nature, being mindful in the garden, there is no telling what you will learn. If you make a lifelong habit of it, I am confident that you will live a fulfilling life.

Unfortunately, the modern world has made it more difficult for us to spend intimate time in nature consciously. We pass through life with an innate hunger for a deep relationship with nature, a hunger that cannot easily be satiated within the confines of our current culture. We are always indoors, and even when we are not, we are rushing around from one place to another, hardly ever even looking up from our cell phones. What us moderners need to remember is that we are still natural creatures of the natural world. We can get a house plant, a succulent, or a kitchen herb placed on the windowsill. We can simply admire the trees in the parking lot when we go to the grocery store—and maybe shop for locally farmed produce while we are there. If we are financially stable and wildly adventurous, we can even go buy property off the grid to become a full-time homesteader. Or do anything in between. There is infinite possibility when considering planting a garden, but I guarantee that, however large or small, the benefits of reminding your physiology of where it came from will be tangible. There is always the opportunity to plant a garden and make nature spend time with you. And do not let space be a problem for you. One pot with one plant or a single packet of seeds is just fine.

As a matter of fact, I think that is a great place for you to start.

And a wonderful place for me to finish.

In a world full of flowers. Some domestic and some wild. All natural. Simple and beautiful.

You are not a poison on the planet. You are one of Mother Earth's most valuable creatures.

Plant a seed. Grow something. Let life happen.

Harmonize with nature. Make your life a song.

Recommended Resources

Food Production

- Charles Dowding, see No-Till
- *Gardening without Poisons* (Book)
- *The Thriving Farmer* (Podcast)

Garden Design

- *California Master Gardener Handbook* (Book)
- *Permaculture: A Designers Manual* (Book)
- *The New Sunset Western Garden: The Ultimate Gardeners Guide* (Book)

No-Till

- Charles Dowding (Instagram, *YouTube), No-Dig: Nurture Your Soil to Grow Better Veg with Less Effort* (Book), *Compost: Transform Waste into New Life* (Book)
- No-Till Farmer (Podcast & Website)
- *Mycelium Running: How Mushrooms Can Help Save the World* (Book)

Plant Health

- *Botany for Gardeners: An Introduction to the Science of Plants* (Book)
- WUCOLS (List of landscape plant water needs by species, can be found online)

References

(1) *Botany for Gardeners: An Introduction to the Science of Plants 3rd Edition-Brian Capon, Timber Press 2010 (p175)*

(2) *Gardening Without Poisons – Beatrice Trum Hunter, Berkeley Medallion Books 1971 (p21)*

(3) *No-Dig: Nurture Your Soil to Grow Better Vegetables with Low Effort – Charles Dowding, Penguin Random House 2022 (p14)*

(4) *Othello – William Shakespeare, Act One, Scene Three, Iago (p56)*

(5) *Rabindranath Tagore, Indian Nobel Prize in Literature Winner, 1913*

(6) *The Gardeners Guide to Better Soil 1st Edition-Gene Longsdon and the other Editors of Organic Gardening, Rodale Press, Inc. 1975 (p9)*

www.ingramcontent.com/pod-product-compliance
Ingram Content Group UK Ltd.
Pitfield, Milton Keynes, MK11 3LW, UK
UKHW050015150425
5457UKWH00033B/9

9 781662 959844